Journey to be

Albert Krassner

Journey to be

Albert Krassner

Edited by Lois Hobson
Veridon Editions
Washington, D.C.

Publishers

Veridon Editions
P.O. Box 70061
Washington, D.C. 20088

ISBN-0-912061-00-6

Printed in Mexico
by Imprenta Madero SA.
Avena 102
Mexico DF.

"I now want to be
Free from cares
To live
And in my own Self... be...."

Acknowledgments

The suggestion to write **Journey to be** came from Swami Muktananda who died on October 2, 1982 before **Journey to be** was completed. The final poem in this book was specially written on the occasion of his death. Quotations from Swami Muktananda's book, **Where are you Going?** have been used throughout **Journey to be,** along with quotes from various traditional scriptures, other enlightened beings, sages and poets.

The concept and creative editing for the book was that of Lois Hobson who saw in my writings the steps and terrain of my journey. Because she understood the journey so well herself, she was able to conceive this presentation, creating order and symmetry out of the hundreds of poems I had written so that this voyage could be enjoyed and shared with others.

The design, photographs, and illustrations were prepared by Arcoiris, a graphic design studio in Guadalajara, Mexico. Their visuals sensitively capture the mood and substance of the poems, adding immeasurably to the total presentation.

To all of the above, I am forever grateful.

Journey to be is based on a search... a search to learn how to live life with greater satisfaction, with greater continuing contentment and ease. It describes an inner journey that begins with day to day observations and reflections, myriad questions for finding logic in living... and finally arrives at an awareness, a level of understanding and consciousness of a higher purpose for living.

It is a journey that has been traveled many times by many others — some who, by their example and writings, left paths and written guidance for others to follow. **Journey to be** makes reference to these previous travelers and acknowledges their contribution in the many quotes used throughout the book.

There will be those who may enjoy **Journey to be** for the verse and graphics alone. I hope there will be those who will enjoy it because they understand and identify with the journey, having experienced themselves the infinite rewards and benefits of learning how... to be.

Contents

I   Wanderings   1

II   Quandaries   25

III   Awarenesses   49

IV   Becoming   73

V   Being   99

Introductory Note

Journey to be is presented in five interrelated but independent chapters, each expressing the dominant place in time of the author's inner growth and development of understanding. Each chapter opens with a poem setting forth the theme for that chapter. Opposite each of these opening poems is a response from a source or sources other than the author. These responses challenge as well as encourage the searcher at each stage of his journey to look beyond the obvious for the answers and guidance he seeks. Quotations from different philosophies and religious references used throughout the book help to highlight the ecumenical nature of the journey and indicate similarities in essential and fundamental teachings even though outer appearances are different.

The searcher begins his journey in the first chapter, **Wanderings,** and moves through levels of unfoldment represented in the chapters — **Quandaries, Awarenesses, Becoming, Being.** The sense of inner bondage and the gradual awakening and freeing of the searcher is graphically portrayed throughout the book by the expanding and contracting lines or grids and symbolically in representations like the butterfly in **Quandaries,** the lone traveler in **Awarenesses,** and the solitary tree and lofty nature scenes in **Chapters IV** and **V.** The tree has long been a symbol for the contemplative and a source of comfort and refuge for the lonely traveler, and so takes on a similar significance for the searcher in this book as well.

Each chapter is very different in tone, mood, and visual presentation. At each juncture of this journey, the searcher himself is different, reflecting at times uncertainty, contradiction, but always a determination to go on and on with the journey he has begun.

Chapters IV and **V** reflect definite breaks into new awarnesses. Often memories of past experience interrupt, but on reflection, the searcher emerges wiser and stronger. As he comes to understand and identify with that mysterious essence... force... strength... love that is found in the unity and oneness of all things, he discovers a greater sense of freedom, a sense of infinity and the Infinite... a sense of being, and thus, a meaning for living.

Chapter I

Wanderings

Many places I did go
Many things I tried to know...
I searched hard, I searched long.

Many probes at life I made
Many consequences made me afraid
But my drive could not be stayed.

"O friend, where are you going?
Where have you come from, and
what are you supposed to do?

You belong to the supreme Truth,
but you have forgotten your origin.
Now it is time
to get back on the main road."

Swami Muktananda

"Without going outside, you may know
the whole world
Without looking through the window,
you may see the ways of heaven.
The farther you go, the less you know.

Thus the sage knows without traveling,
He sees without looking,
He works without doing."

Lao Tsu

3

There comes a time
in everyone's life
to reflect on one's self...
to ask what has happened and why
and where am I
relative to the time that's passed
and the situation I am now in?

   Does it make sense
to go my way as before?
Is it time to do something more
or different or in another way,
to refresh myself
to take a holiday?

   It seems as natural as can be
given these feelings at hand
to seek that difference
to make my life expand.

   Should I venture forward, outward
in all directions
begin to have flings
with different people, places, things?

   Well, it all starts out easy
with self to discuss
and sometimes things happen...
people stray
sometimes settling...
for come what may.

What is right
What is wrong...
The question is
Where do I belong?

4

Is it all blind
My way to find?

I'm at the crossroads.
Where to go?
Signs don't show!

I have seen glories in this world
and I believe there are more
I have viewed vistas
I had never dreamed before.

Friendships over the world
plans beyond my place
sights beyond my view
each with challenges all through...

Yet in all that is out there still
There is much more that I can will!

I have seen glories in this world
and I believe there are more...

Standing on a bluff
overlooking the sea,
breathing in the lovely day
and the gentle wind.
Bright foliage lining the walk
to the short stretch of sandy beach
where a few stray seabirds are
in sight...

The sun's warmth touching
everything around,
flowing through me,
blending me in as part of the scene...

Waiting for the sun to set
its day of play
with the sea all spent.

   Slowly the light wiggles
over the wavering water
to spend the night
beyond the ocean tide.

Watching the sun set at sea...

...I have viewed vistas
I had never dreamed before...

...soothing, steaming waters
descending from a volcanic crest
high in the mountains...
bouncing over beaten bedrock...
indifferent to time and turmoil...

...enormous canyons...
carved out by wind and water
over eons of time —
nature's monuments...
majestic, awesome...

...Friendships over the world
plans beyond my place
sights beyond my view
each with challenges all through...

In a strange land
Nothing is strange.

Differences are only outward
What we wear
What we eat
How we speak.

The central scene
Always the same...
People seeking their lives
As we seek ours.

Desperation, frustration, hopelessness
Feelings found in people everywhere...
But which is more tearing —
Poverty... or a poor spirit?

In a strange land
Nothing is strange.

...Yet in all that is out there still
There is much more that I can will!

At Prides Crossing a day ago,
I visited by chance a home by the sea
where my dreams from the past
moved up to the fore...

thoughts of the sea
rose up in my mind
childhood memories
days of quiet... of ease

to live by the sea
to hear the waves, see their roll
to feel the throbbing inside
in touch with my soul

walking alone
breathing deeply
feeling one with nature
and the endless view
and the smell of the sea

My heart was full of dreams unformed
...all brought in by the sea
at Prides Crossing a day ago.

In the greatest togetherness
We stand alone.

Longing to be
In touch
Aware
At ease
Ourselves.

Wanting love
Wanting ourselves
Wanting...

The mood is loneliness
So much around... no one to share
Past glories
New dreams...

All's well... but not
Can one be well
Feeling incomplete?

Going around, nowhere to be
But to be...

My eyes introduce my soul to the new day!

I cannot grasp reality
So I watch the stray thoughts
Slip into my soul
As the sun rises.

Dark trees outlined by a low lit sky
Cloud streams gently caressed by light
Strands of red, blue
Melding into white...
The day begins before the sun arrives.

The birds are up
Their hour to rise
And have their say...
The day has come.

The sun peeks through the blue
Above and around
Promises of goodness
Without a sound...
The day begins.

"To him whose vigorous thought
keeps pace with the sun,
the day is a perpetual morning."

Thoreau

Bulbous clouds of white
stand suspended
in an azure sky —
stacking threats of thunder heads...
scattered, shapeless, seething forms
screening the shining sun.

Up and up and up they move —
maybe to crash
cascading ice and heavy rain...
maybe to pass gently to another place.

Clouds within us are just the same —
enormous energy encased inside
steaming forth wonders
only man can make —
occasionally careening, climaxing, clashing
in callous wake.

"...and God divided
the light from the darkness.
And God called
the light day
and the darkness
He called Night."

Genesis, Ch.I

The still night...

Bright stars
Twinkling down
Through wisps of cloud
Feeling the quiet.

It is night's time to be
Its dark purity
Assuring that all is
As created to be.

The night...
Still
Stilling.

"Of his mercy
he hath made for you
the night and the day...."

The Koran, Ch. 28

There is no down when I rise each day
The night's dragons in my dreams I slay.

Demons of the night gone by
Strewn beyond my cares.

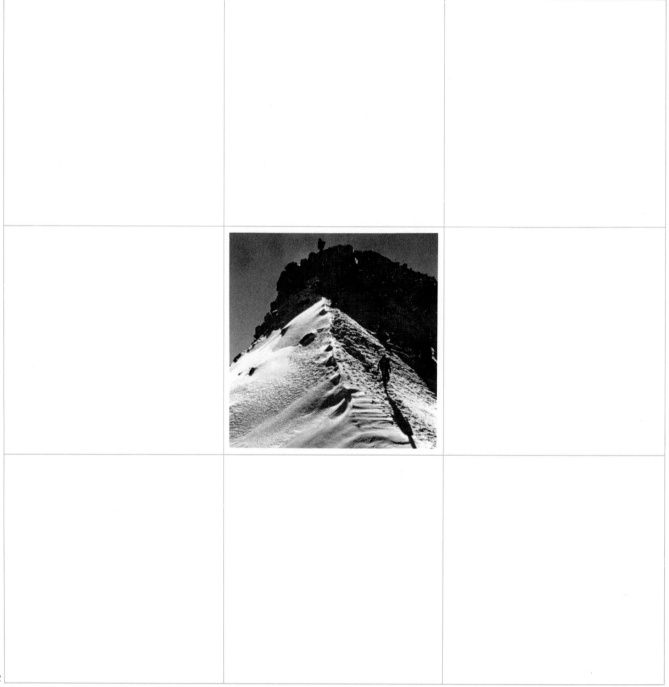

Rounding the bend
One must slow down...

Change pace for a while
Though it's not clear what's ahead
And comfort's now behind.

It doesn't matter not to see
What matters is to be inclined
To accept such times must be.

Slowing down is right to do
Even coasting for a while
With only confidence to see one through.

Moving forward... with control
Looking back will only brake
Future happiness... the goal.

The view ahead will surely come
For life has its bends for all, not some
For all of us... who wish to be.

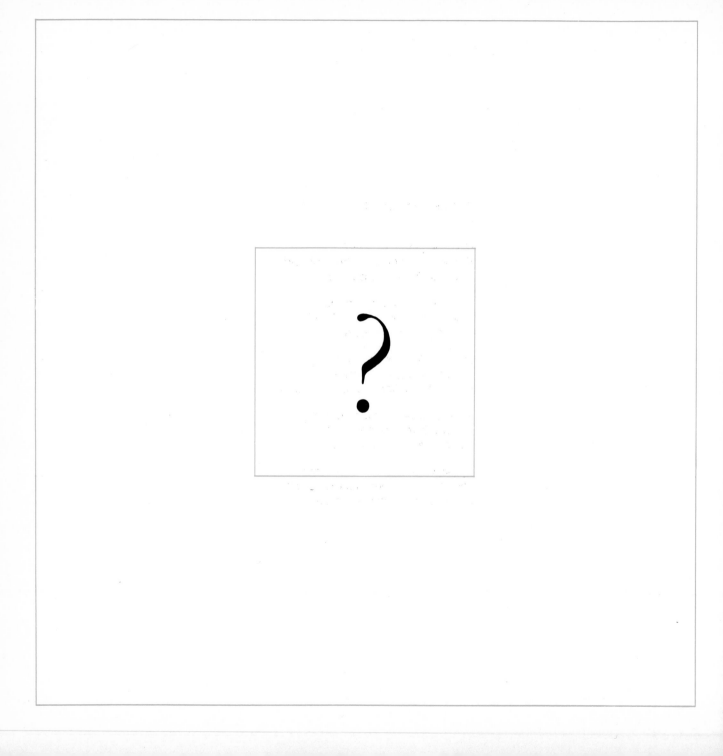

Chapter II

Quandaries

Who am I
Why care to know
Why should I try
Why think so

What is my role
Here on earth
Just to live and die...
No other worth

?

"What is man,
that thou art mindful of him?
And the son of man,
that thou visitest him?"

Psalm 8:4

"What is it, then, that makes a human being unique?
Only a human being has the capacity to know
the divine Consciousness vibrating within him.
Only a human being has the ability to experience his identity with God.
That is why we must use this human life to discover who we are.

The Indian Scriptures say
that only one who contemplates the questions

  'Who am I?'
  'Why was I born?'
  'Who created me?'
  'What am I supposed to do?'
is truly human".

Muktananda

Mountain and dale
Should this prevail
Or should I be
With sand and sea?

Where to dwell
For spirit to swell
Where to live
My time to give—

Mountain views
Fields and trees
Running streams
Footpaths and quiet roads

Lakes and ponds
Caves and caverns
For undisturbed serenity
Like a bird on the wing?

¿?

Where to go for joy
For ease and love and God?

How do I nurture my spirit?
How do I recognize its need?
Is it only mind and body
To regularly feed?

What about the spirit?
How does it get its due?
Should it be forsaken
This important part of you?

Where do I draw the line?
How do I myself define?
Why can't what I want for me
Be brought to be?

Do we conform with form
Or do we something higher obey?
There are several theories -
Who has the say?

What is the point?
What is the goal?
To be with the body
Or satisfy the soul?

?

What should I do?

Where do I go?

What do I do now?
What I have already done
must not be my conceit
nor regrets my score
What is left undone
seems only all the more.

What can I do?
This I must explore...
With patience... and ease of course
so not to force...

Let me be and do and go...

What can I learn?

What more can I know?

What can I learn?

What should I do?

I know that it's not all I see
That there is much, much more
That lies beyond me...

Where do I go?

What more can I know?

The need
to be
FREE
burns
in me!

What can I do?

I'm caught in a trap
can't get out
can't even shout!

What can I do?

?

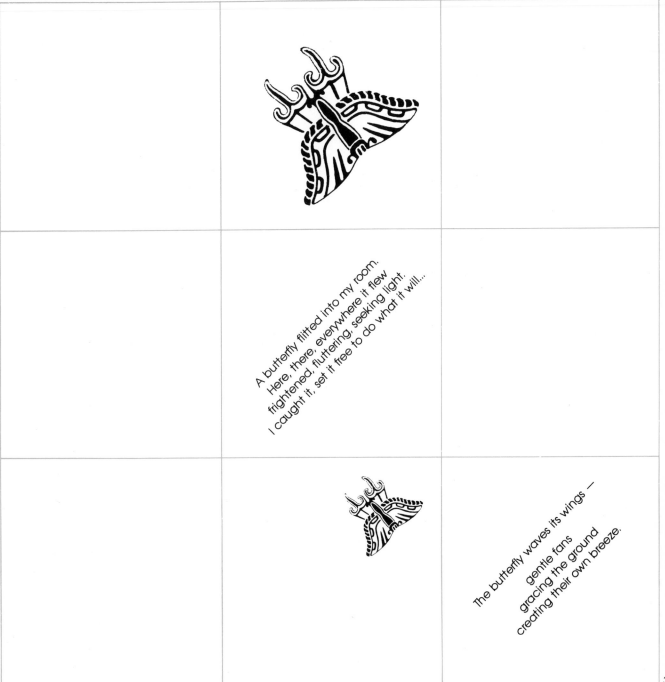

A butterfly flitted into my room.
Here, there, everywhere it flew
frightened, fluttering, seeking light.
I caught it, set it free to do what it will...

The butterfly waves its wings —
gentle fans
gracing the ground
creating their own breeze.

Katydids
out there, somewhere-

I listen
maybe see
imagine a movement
hear a change in their key.

Incessant sounds
resounding everywhere
filling the air.

Are they many?
Are they few?
How do they make their tune?
Not knowing no longer will do!

Katydids
out there, somewhere-

I'm compelled to learn about you
the why and how of your nocturnal song
filling the air
resounding everywhere
...without a care!

"Because half a dozen grasshoppers under a fern
make the field ring with their importunate chink...
do not imagine that those who make the noise are the only inhabitants of the field...."

Edmund Burke

There's a sadness sneaking in...

I am sad
I want to cry
My sadness
No one else's.

I can't share it
It's mine alone —
Should I feel this way?
I do.

I'll look away
It will pass
...to return again?

Is this part of life —
To feel hurt, then go on again?

Maybe...
I'm part of life... and I'm sad.

Oh Lord, why?
Why life with imperfection
Personal, private... imperfection?

And love —
Going forth in so many forms
And life —
So much imperfection...

Pleasure and pain
When these two come into play
Which one should hold sway?

When one seems the best
The other arises, starts to test.

Which should it be?

I tried to find where the answer lies
Was it my system of values to revise?...

Teach me to be free from cares
that should not concern
Teach me to be easy as I yearn...

Is it a grand illusion
that we can share our lives with another - totally
that another can be near and yet not fully there
that perfect pairing with another can be found?

Is it just part of the human condition
a natural deficiency —to experience nearness—
but completeness... an impossibility?

Is it a grand illusion
that we can share our lives with another - totally
that another can be near and yet not fully there
that perfect pairing with another can be found?

Is it just part of the human condition
a natural deficiency —to experience nearness—
but completeness... an impossibility?

I'm a loner — apparently
Doing my thing — purposefully
Do I want to? Do I agree?
It doesn't seem to matter...
It's beyond me.

"If you find no better or equal
on life's road,
go alone!"

Dhammapada

?!

• •

"Don't take yourself seriously!"

?

•

What does this mean?
How can this be?
Am I a nonentity?

This can't be so
I surely count
Are you telling me
I'm not the whole amount?

Okay, so I accept
Maybe even relieved somehow
I'm to act
But also to share the bow!

Who else plays a role in my show?
If it's not all me
Where else do the credits go?

"There's no one else
Who can play your role.
Each is his own actor
Only a part of the Whole."

Walk in the woods
Follow a path
Stray somewhat
Make your own swath.

Look here and there
See what can be found...
Feel your soul
on untrampled ground!

Take the time to say "Hello"...

Once in a while, someone startles us, changes our mind.

It often happens by surprise...
Bells can sound...
It's exciting, even profound...

!

when someone from without
starts a happening
within!

I've been struggling so long with sin
I find it hard to get rid of this terrible stuff!
  It's really easy to recognize —
But how to live with it and not self despise?
To look away and carry on
Hoping that it will soon be gone!

Oh no, It's not that way!
Sin, it seems, only wants to stay
What do I do?
I want so much to learn!
  Now I've been told
I can give my sins away!
If only I could believe this to be!

Whom do I trust, become allied?
With what God do I become tied?

?

God to know
Yes, no, never?
The means...
However?

Chapter III

Awarenesses

My life is changing and I don't care
I am now... coming to be
Alone with myself... and free.

I'm at home when I am there
Not to roam when I don't care
But to be and be and be
With myself... internally.

Faces the same, but different
Places the same, but different
I am one with all of me
As I was... meant to be.

Yet to change
And become... more of me.

"Muktananda: *...This is a question of understanding.*
You have already realized God;
however, you are not aware of it.

Question: *Can I become aware?*
Muktananda: *That awareness is what you have to*
attain. It is just as if you had ten
dollars in your pocket but forgot it
was there and said you had no money.
Then you put your hand in your pocket
and said, 'Oh, I found the money.' What
would you mean when you said that you
had found the money? It was already
there. You found what you already had."

"At the heart of this phenomenal world,
within all its changing forms,
dwells the unchanging Lord.

So, go beyond the changing,
and, enjoying the inner,
cease to take for yourself
what to others are riches."

The Upanishads

When I was young
I did not see
The wonderful things
That were shown to me.

I did not understand
When others tried
To help me appreciate
All the glories outside -
    birds and flowers
    music and starry nights...

But today
I am aglow!

I now know
That what is truly true
That what is glorious outside -
Comes first from the inside view.

Flowers all around
Catch my eye as I run -
Stop! I feel inside...

    see their beauty
    the colors galore
    the graceful flow
    row upon row.

    each - in glory to God
    each - so perfect and right
    each - a wondrous delight!

The bright sky unfolds
in an unending blue...
nothing to interrupt the eye,
nothing to interrupt the imagination!

I am seeing more each day...

A solitary bird on the beach, its head held high on feathered shaft...
a bulging body on skinny clawed feet.
Tail feathers fluttering in the wild ocean breeze,
preparing to fly away to somewhere...

I am seeing more each day...

A lone flower flinching in the wind...
its red running loud against the yellow faded into pale by the sun.
Dark and alluring the flower's pistil
beckons the bee from its dull run of the day.

I am seeing more each day...

The ocean wave rolling to the shore, shedding its white mane in the sand.
Draining and dribbling, it vanishes into the reservoir below
to be returned for further splash and play.

I am seeing more each day...

The glistening sun rising in the sky at early morn...
light playing on scattered clouds, turning grey to white, yellow, red.
The morning blue, holding images for my mind to play as it may.

I am feeling more each day...

Sensing strength to stay my thoughts away from drift
and where I do not wish to be.

I am more each day...

Seeing, feeling, sensing more of myself
in the ongoing scenes of my everyday.

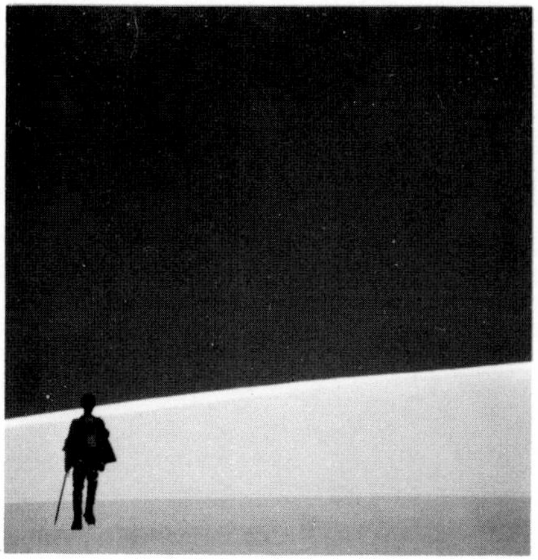

I'm a witness to this scene
Of change in me
I watch as best I can
For its meaning to see...

When I try for perspective
It helps -
But chance often intervenes
And a different destiny I see...

So much is a mystery...

"To every thing there is a season,
and a time to every purpose
under the heaven...".

Ecclesiastes 3:1

Only through pain and suffering
To know
Can we grow
Strange as it seems
These are the means.

Isn't this a bedevilment for sure
That only unhappiness
        can unhappiness cure?

Life's so full of disappointments...

We go on wondering
Bedeviled, befuddled, forlorn
Allowing our tears to remain torn.

Am I strong enough now
to bring you warmth, love,
                    compassion—
to help you to love life...?

I'm torn between two worlds -
to go where I've already been
seeing what I've already seen
or going for what... I've started to glean.

Getting upset
Getting annoyed...
I'm not there yet!

"How to escape from this world I'm in?"
The cry of my mind caught on a thing!

Ego... you made me high
and laid me low!

We are trained to think this and that
Much of which keeps us where we're at —
Caught and tied
To appearances outside...

Now I know —
  nothing's compelling
  no tragedy's befelling
  just my ego yelling!

Pity man
Man — what a pity!
Caught up
In life's nitty — gritty!

Can't see the larger play
Thinks it's only the mind to obey!

mind mind mind mind mind mind mind mind mind mind
ego ego ego ego ego ego ego ego ego
mind mind mind mind mind mind mind mind
ego ego ego ego ego ego ego
mind mind mind mind mind
ego ego ego ego
mind mind mind
ego ego
mind

We cannot with the finite mind
the infinite find!

Don't get complicated
    please, please
Keep my life one of
    ease, ease
Scenes all around me
    tease, tease
My peace and tranquillity
    not to appease
Keep things simple
Everything a breeze
No now or later difficulties
    please, please.

Soar...on an inner breeze

I now want to be
  free from cares —
  to live
    and in my own Self... be.
It's not easy to do —
  old cares have their ways
  of coming back to intrude
  continuing their replays.
I'll resist as best I can
  to be... today
  outside of cares
  of yesterday.

So many times we have a chance
to discontinue
the downward
dance

and experience...
the inside
hum.

If we could see ourselves —
all the joys inside
We would see we really can't stray
from man's destiny
We would live our lives content...
our allotment of time well spent.

The Hebrew prayer
"Modeh ahnee" – I give thanks –
I pray each morn
just around the crack of dawn.

One day at a time — just one
This is the rhythm
I've begun.

"The old order changeth,
yielding place to new..."

Tennyson

Chapter IV

Becoming

A spell of love
I found
Not in this or that
But in everything around.
I found out that God,
the Love in this world,
Flows from me!
I became enraptured
Captivated by this discovery!

*"...for behold,
the kingdom of God
is within you..."*

Luke 17:21

GOD IS LOVE GOD IS LOVE GOD IS LOVE
GOD IS LOVE GOD IS LOVE GOD IS LOVE
GOD IS LOVE GOD IS LOVE GOD IS LOVE
GOD IS LOVE GOD IS LOVE GOD IS LOVE
GOD IS LOVE GOD IS LOVE GOD IS LOVE
GOD IS LOVE GOD IS LOVE GOD IS LOVE
GOD IS LOVE GOD IS LOVE GOD IS LOVE
GOD IS LOVE GOD IS LOVE GOD IS LOVE
GOD IS LOVE GOD IS LOVE GOD IS LOVE
GOD IS LOVE GOD IS LOVE GOD IS LOVE
GOD IS LOVE GOD IS LOVE GOD IS LOVE
GOD IS LOVE GOD IS LOVE GOD IS LOVE
GOD IS LOVE GOD IS LOVE GOD IS LOVE
GOD IS LOVE GOD IS LOVE GOD IS LOVE
GOD IS LOVE GOD IS LOVE GOD IS LOVE
GOD IS LOVE GOD IS LOVE GOD IS LOVE

*"God dwells within you
as you."*

Muktananda

It was just like magic
It took me by surprise
Something came over me
Before my very eyes.

I felt a surging
Coming into me fast
A sense of euphoria
I wanted to last.

I felt a comfort
I didn't know before
I discovered a wonder —
Love at my core.

*"Having perceived It
by His grace,
remain solitary,
tranquil,
without desires,
and without any attachment...."*

Guru Gita

*"For by grace
are ye saved
through faith;
and that not of yourselves;
it is the gift of God."*

Ephesians 2:8

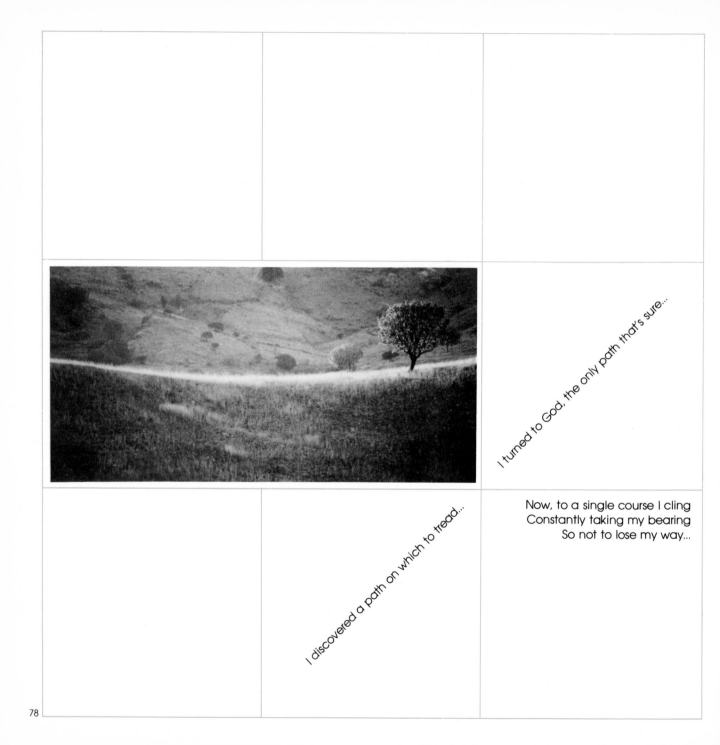

I turned to God, the only path that's sure...

I discovered a path on which to tread...

Now, to a single course I cling
Constantly taking my bearing
So not to lose my way...

There is no one way
For one to do
To be oneself
To oneself be true.

Life is not marked
With signs that show
Paths to follow
Or ways to go.

What there is
Is for each to find
How to be in touch
The Self to find.

*"Like the moon
slipping from behind a cloud
and shining on the earth
is the man who,
once foolish,
has determined to be wise."*

Dhammapada

If we could see what is true
we would see no differences
between me and you.

We would see
that we are one and the same
indistinguishable...
except by name.

That all are brothers under the skin
members of the Divine family
in which all are kin.

Why so many forms
When it is only One
That people seek
Under the sun?

Why the differences
In how people pray
When it is the same call
They seek to obey?

Why does this happen?
We are all the same inside —
That what appears outside
Does this sameness hide.

"Shema Israel"
Hear O Israel
the Lord our God
the Lord is One.

Hebrew prayer

Only form deceives...

And beyond form
a greater Essence sits
knowing everything is
only a manifestation of This.

Our body, our mind
is all part of the flow
we come and go
we rise and set...

to rise again.

Now coming into fruition
is my delayed recognition
that our human condition
is just another rendition.

Don't know how come or what for
our lives from before
are part of our core.

Each time we play a particular role
nothing's the same... only the soul
eternally under God's control.

*"How many births
have I known
without knowing
the builder
of this body!
How many births
have I looked
for him!"*
Dhammapada

Whatever we do
however we view
it's a carrying through
of other times we knew.

Very, very weird
yet, not to be feared
just another explanation
that in other lifetimes
we've been reared.

Stars splashing across the sky
like specks of crystal
strewn across the black
mysteriously silent
holding secrets
for all alike!

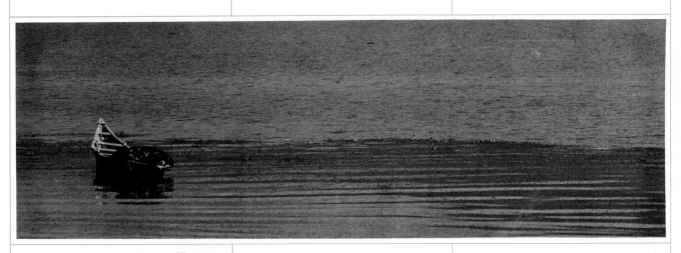

Silence...
Near at hand
Standing aside
Waiting to command.

Some listen
To this special friend inside
...Seldom interrupting.

Become aware
Of this silent friend.
Look for it everywhere
Enjoy the marvels
Of its private company!

I must let go	... I know
It's so hard to do	... Why so?
I've worked so hard	... So you say
What will do?	... Take it day by day
I know I should	... It's time to do
My reasons are sound	... They are, they are
Will they prevail?	... Why will they not?
What will I do?	... Why fear to know?
Will I be better off?	... Compared to what?
I'm aware of the need	... I understand this need
I will try each day	... I know I must
Trust in God	... It's the only way
I will free up!	... And have faith... to be!

Seeing a thought dart in and out
Watching as it comes about
Amazed to see this inner flow
How my thoughts can come and go.

It's a special kind of show
How it happens - I don't know!
Can it be that what I see
Is just a form of energy?

Energy moving mysteriously
Forming, going, doing endlessly...

It comes from within, this call
It comes without a sound...
Louder each day...

I felt a voice inside that said...

I am the greater You
that you can be
the better you
the happier man
what you'd like to be
and can!

The challenge is... to be!
And from expectations - free!

I want to do more
and more and more
Doing what I feel
Feeling what I do.

I want to keep it up
Make it last and last...

This inner flow
Full and deep inside
Makes me glow!

We're not the Doer
We're not the One
Who makes things happen
Who makes things run.

It s not left to us
To say and do
To act as best we know
To make things come true.

It should be left to God
Define God as you may
Who is the Doer
Who has the last say.

*"...the Father
that dwelleth in me,
he doeth the works."*

John 14:10

*"... a knower of Truth
considers
all the actions he does
to be non - action..."*

Guru Gita

It's all God's play, anyway!

God,
I'm with You now
I feel Your grace
I feel Your warmth
I feel Your love.

I'm now aware
That I am You
That You are in my form
That You are in my spirit.

No more apart
I am free...
Aware of You...
I'm with You now.

"In returning and rest
you shall be saved;
in quietness and in trust
shall be your strength."

Isaiah 30:15

Chapter V

Being

One step at a time
Just to start...
One experience at a time
Each one true...
One moment at a time
Each filled with bliss...

This is the ultimate
I'm now sure of this.

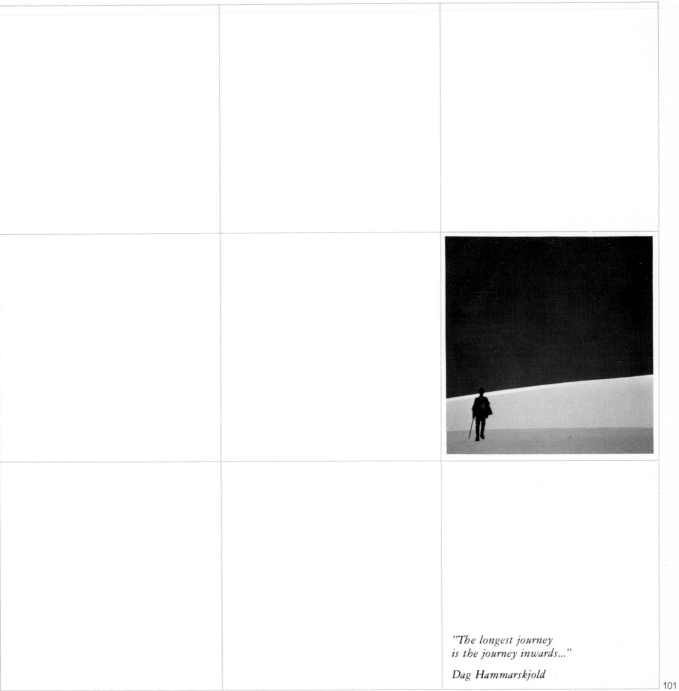

*"The longest journey
is the journey inwards..."*

Dag Hammarskjold

How to simplify my life?
What is there to shed?
What can be dismissed?
What will be instead?

What should I seek?
This I investigate
I know it's not a thing
That can ever satiate...

These quests were false
Right from the start -
The answers came through
When I realized - nothing's apart.

How to simplify my life...

not regret, only review
not regret like I used to do
rehashing what happened—
    starting to stew
allowing past events
    to boil and brew...

never acting over-zealously...

for others to spare
I'll try to forbear
until it's clear
they wish to share...

stop thinking of disasters
that have not taken place-
experiencing traumas
I don't have to face...

What should I seek...

"Those who know do not talk
Those who talk do not know.

Keep your mouth closed
Guard your senses
Temper your sharpness
Simplify your problems
Mask your brightness
Be at one with the dust of the earth
This is primal union.

He who has achieved this state
Is unconcerned with friends
    and enemies
With good and harm,
    with honor and disgrace.
    This therefore
Is the highest state of man."

Lao Tsu

The rising sun
Peeking - over - the - earth's - surface - as - I - run

A - few - more - steps - and - up - it - pops -
So - exciting - my - running - almost - stops!

The sky lights up
Before the sun appears
Stars begin to fade
The moon pales
Soon - altogether out of sight.

The brightness in the sky now complete
This change from night to day - an awesome feat!

Come on, Day,
bring your wares!

I'll take
whatever
you've
got!

Come on, Day,
I
want
you
to
star!

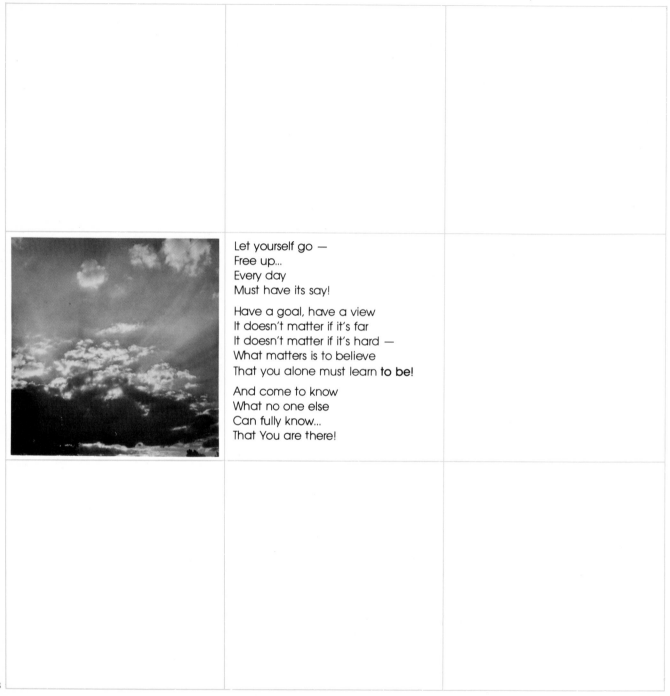

Let yourself go —
Free up...
Every day
Must have its say!

Have a goal, have a view
It doesn't matter if it's far
It doesn't matter if it's hard —
What matters is to believe
That you alone must learn **to be**!

And come to know
What no one else
Can fully know...
That You are there!

I think I know myself
 but I shall look for more
I think that I am true
 and this — I must always be.

What I do now cannot be judged
 by me alone
What I want cannot be
 the test alone.

There is wisdom in this world —
 mine, not alone.

Feelings and thoughts
 are only parts of me
Faith, above all,
 is what is most for me.

I'm moving forward...
I feel it in the air...

To want to share
but from sharing shy

To sense joys
but not them fully feel

To love
but not trust that it's real...

The time will come
to test what is true —
whether to give love
and receive it too
whether to continue in the clouds
or move into the blue.

In all I behold that's beautiful
You are there.

In all that captures
My thoughts of love
You are there.

In all that gives me hope and joy
You are there.

It is something I cannot explain
It is something I wish to feel —
Feelings of love all over.

This is the way it should be...
Loving life, having hope, yearning...
To be.

If I see you as God
And if it were the same for you
Can it be imagined
All that we are, can be, can do?

Can we imagine
Understand to some degree
What can be accomplished
If this we see?

To move beyond our minds
A higher consciousness obey —
Where will it lead
Who can say?

"Surrender yourself humbly;
then you can be trusted
to care for all things.

Love the world as your own self;
then you can truly care
for all things".

Lao Tsu

"...Do not think that God is only in your heart.

You should be able to recognize Him in every garden,
in every forest,
in every house,
and in every person.

You should be able to see Him in your destination,
in all stages of your journey,
and in all your fellow pilgrims.

You should be able see Him on every path,
in every philosophy,
and in every group.

You should be able to see Him in all acts,
in all deeds,
in all thoughts and feelings,
and in all expressions of them.

You should be able to recognize Him
not only in inner lights,
but also in the lights that you see
in the outer world.

All colors
and even the darkness are the same Being.
If you really love Him,
if you want to find His love
and be blessed by it,
then see Him in every corner of the universe."

Muktananda

It is a mystery that it has to be...
Meditation... done regularly!

My thoughts flow into rest...

easing down
being still

The soft air blows
The ocean rolls
I'm at one with the sea...

This is meditation for me.

Meditation...

If it is from the mind
To become free
How can the mind agree?

Most people say they can't
By itself the mind will not recant!

Great beings have this mastery won
Basking always in the inner sun.

Go inside...
From without,
       the mind is the great divide!

"Sit very quietly in your chair;
then turn within and try to see
who watches your thoughts from inside.
    If you keep watching in that way,
you will come to know the Self...
    As you keep contemplating the Self,
as you keep trying to understand the Self,
it will reveal itself to you.
    So turn within.
Look for that inner knower.
God is in your heart...."

Muktananda

May my faith
flow inside
like the greatest sea.

May I feel its flow
witness its happening
forever.

May it show
that I reflect God's presence
in thought and deed -
that whatever happens -
my faith... always to stay.

I've become involved with the One
The One Being with whom life began
God, the Love of everyone —
I know this affair will never be done.

"...the realized soul is merged in the highest Self. Day and night, wherever he may be, the realized being delights in his identity with the Supreme Being."

Guru Gita

125

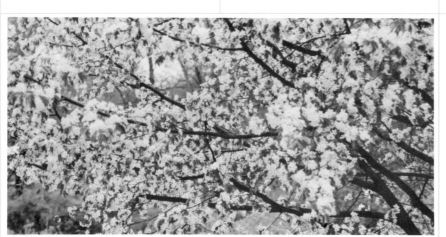

The season is magically in change
trees and flowers doing their thing
buddings becoming apparent
silently in praise they sing.

Morning skies crisp and clear
long dark evenings bid good bye
cold in the air disappearing
shouting out "It's spring!"

All life becomes affected
gladness and newness all about
nature's smile is in all things
spring in me, too, is coming out!

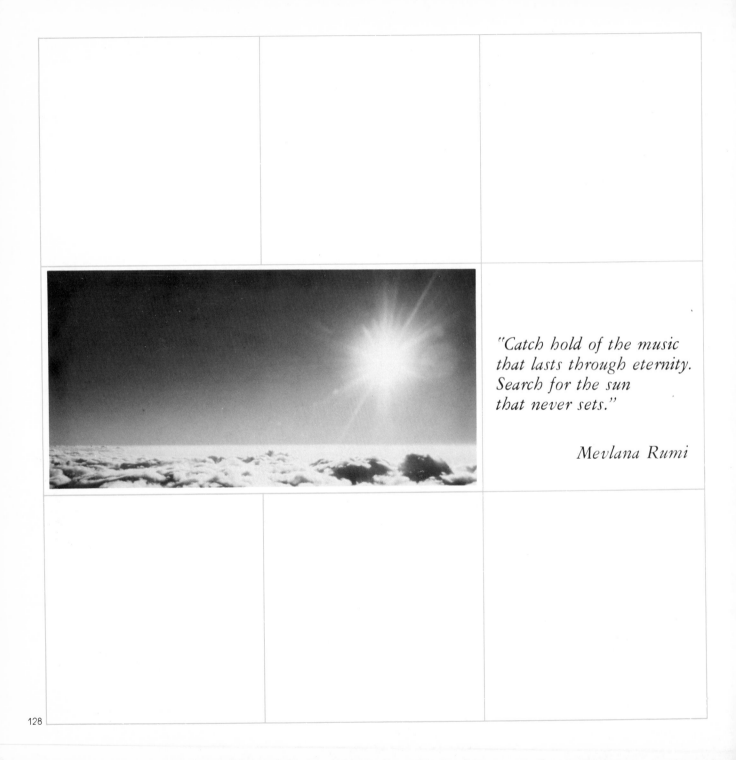

*"Catch hold of the music
that lasts through eternity.
Search for the sun
that never sets."*

Mevlana Rumi

"...the pure Self alone.
Dwelling in the heart of all,
it is the lord of all,
the seer of all,
the source and goal of all.

It is not outer awareness,
It is not inner awareness,
Nor is it a suspension of awareness.
It is not knowing,
It is not unknowing,
Nor is it knowingness itself.
It can neither be seen nor understood,
It cannot be given boundaries.
It is ineffable and beyond thought.
It is indefinable.
It is known only through becoming It.
It is the end of all activity,
silent and unchanging,
the supreme good,
one without a second.
It is the real Self.
It, above all, should be known."

The Upanishads

"The Gift"

On hearing the news of
Swami Muktananda's death

October 2, 1982

He made me aware of the Self
That was his gift
Without this awareness
My life seemed to drift.

He gave me this gift
Without any cost
Showing a path
Where I would not get lost.

He helped me see God
In all that I did
Before Muktananda
God was hid.

He illumined the way
For me to see
To discover that God
Was inside of me.

A loving experience
I came to feel
Stilling my mind
For God to reveal.

He made me aware of the Self
That was his gift...

He gave me this gift...
Without any cost.